Smallman - Making sense of Business

David Smallman

A simple handbook that will help you make sense of business using stories and thoughts from 55 years of experience on my Life's Highway.

Table of Contents

Foreword

The name David Smallman is absolutely associated with the words Experience, Knowledge, Advice and, last but by no means least, **BUSINESS!**

David's paper *"It's the order - stupid"* (written during the financial downturn of 2008) was, and still is, required reading for all those wishing to build success into their business.

With many interests, David brings a wealth of knowledge to the table. He writes on business and is perhaps best known for his series *"150 words that should make sense in your business"*, a series which has formed the starting point for this book.

David's five decades of experience have encompassed worldwide travel (63 countries), deep learning and teaching (from start-ups to multinationals), and informative writing and broadcasting relentlessly focusing on how to help his clients and audience "make sense of business".

My experience with David started when I worked economic development in the United States, on the Mississippi Gulf Coast. My agency engaged

Pathfinder Team Consulting who brought a different approach to problem solving and business strategy by utilizing a stable of accomplished business advisors in multiple disciplines who were able to properly approach the issues in a Team concept. That first experience extended for many years in multiple states.

Wherever he has gone, and whoever he has mentored, David has proved to be an effective and trusted advisor.

Having retired from management of Pathfinder Team Consulting, David has actively maintained his relationships. He is keen to ensure that former clients have continued access to consulting advice, both in the private and public sectors in the U.S. and around the World.

I can personally speak to David's impact in the USA, where he quickly became a much respected and resourceful adviser in assisting diverse business clients that varied from local economic development organisations, to the State Government in Louisiana, the Great Oklahoma City Chamber of Commerce, and the Delaware Prosperity Partnership, not to mention private sector clients in states including Texas, Alabama, Georgia, Pennsylvania, Massachusetts, and

Florida. It was through many such interactions that I developed a solid personal and professional respect for, and relationship with, David.

When you add the above to his work in South America, Asia, and the Middle East - as well as in his homeland of the UK for an array of clients in both the public and private sectors – it's not hard to understand that David has a wealth of constructive advice to give on the development of successful enterprises.

However, given all of that if asked for one word to describe David Smallman----it's *integrity*.

Michael J Olivier
Gulfport, Mississippi

Tributes

A number of clients and business colleagues from across the years and around the World were asked to give 3 words that summarized their relationship with David and those things that he brought to his work.

Supportive-Enthusiastic-Collaborative.

Andrew Hodgson–Lancaster England

Thoughtful-Rigorous-Resilient.

Don Pierson-Baton Rouge Louisiana

Sage-Universal-Considered.

Bob Donnelly-Aberdeen Scotland

Solutions-Pragmatic-Relentless.

Jim Shankle-Johnson Arkansas

Passion-Focus-Integrity.

Glen Dove-Glasgow Scotland

Insightful-Collaborative-Supportive.

Debbie Mullins—Knoxville Tennessee

Mentor-Inspiring-Considerate.

David Bull-Zhujiang China

Enlightening-Entertaining-Enigmatic.

John Voorhorst-Pinckney Michigan.

Frank-Boisterous-Engaging.

Georgia Gibson-St Ives England

Insightful-Mentor-Instructive.

Richard JR Reed-Slidell Louisiana

Acumen-Focused-Cognitive.

Mike Roach-Sao Paulo Brazil

Credible-Ardent-Foundational.

W Kurt Foreman- Wilmington Delaware

Connaissance-Experience-Comprehension.

Marc Dessenne – Lille France

Dynamic-Inspiring-Sage.

Angel Adrian – New Orleans Louisiana

Connected-Entrepreneurial-Unstoppable.

Andrew Millar – London England

Authors Note

A decade ago, when the idea for this small handbook was first muted by friend of mine in New Orleans, JR Reed, I was skeptical that a) anyone would be interested and b) if I would find enough content!

I was at the time not only still travelling extensively on business but working on building up a following on a business radio show based in the UK.

As the following on the show grew it led me to writing more and having articles published in magazines and newspapers, I realized that people were interested in the stories and thoughts that I had recorded privately over the years from working with folks around the World.

I am no academic and thus these writings are in simple day to day language which is easy to understand and will often be a reminder to readers of things that are obvious, but often forgotten, or express a known idea in a different way that is more relevant to your current situation. I would encourage you to use the space at the end of each piece and between the lines of each thought to make notes as you go along where you can reinforce common experiences, or you pick up on an idea that you might want to share with others later.

I don't for one minute expect every reader to get something out of each and every one of the stories or thoughts, but I do believe that everyone will find something here which resonates and that can be put to good effect in your business as you too travel on Life's Highway.

If you would like to discuss any of the issues raised in these pages you can easily contact me on:
david@smallmanon.biz
LinkedIn.com/in/davidfsmallman, @SmallmanOnBiz.

Finally, to all those who have commented on my time working with them, thank you. Its only when you see these words in black and white that you realize that we can all have a positive impact on others which is outside of our vison; be that today or in the past.

Part 1 – Stories

1)   A Fatal Shot?

The bird is one of the Creators greatest pieces of engineering, intricate in design yet using only air it reaches incredible heights.

It comes in all shapes and sizes, is colourful to look at and fascinating in flight, much like any business.

And the same as the bird however intricate the design of your product or service you need the air of sales in order stay aloft let alone reach the heights of success. But remember that however high it might fly every bird is vulnerable to a single shot.

Then its intricate design, size or colour is no longer of help it's only a question of the speed of its fall.

What single shot would be fatal to your business?

Lack of orders comes in all shapes and sizes market forces, management changes, poor customer service, lack of cost control etc.

What is your sales strategy to stay aloft?

2) A reasonable expense or is it bribery?

Reputable organisations around the world have compliance rules for their staff about offering or accepting "gifts".

This can include simple things like taking an alcoholic drink at a meal and in some cases the meal itself.

Many would say that's draconian; but it is borne out of a 21st century business culture where greater transparency is called for at all levels.

Most western democracies have laws that cover "correct commercial behaviour"

Yet there are many cultures in which – for a "fee" - an arrangement can be made to ensure that your offer will be accepted by your customer. That "fee" is often paid to somebody within the client and often close to if not at the top.

Maybe it's that you view these inducements or incentives as a reasonable expense; perhaps the cost of doing business.

Two definitions of bribery are "inducement" and "incentive".

Is your business worth the risk?

3)   Annoying Phone calls?

How often do you refuse to take a call in your business when the caller asks specifically for you?

Frequently?

However, I assume you always ring back and reply to their message.

No?

Sometime ago I called a former client, to be informed that he was in but on the phone (this device used as a way of getting you to leave a message is very transparent) I left my details and requested a call back.

I unsuccessfully repeated the call three times.

Recently at an industry function he acknowledged that I had called jokingly adding he hadn't called back because he "was very busy" and had assumed I was trying to sell him some further consulting work.

"No" I said, "I had a business friend who asked if I knew anybody who supplied what you make – but it OK I have introduced them to somebody else" Return your calls!

4)   Are you ON it?

Do you work ON or IN your business?

Working IN your business assumes your business is "established" and focuses on "running" the business. It's buying the materials, managing the people, and delivering the service.

Working ON your business is organising the finances, studying new markets, planning the growth, executing your plan, training others, and developing continuity.

Too often business owners and executives place daily emphasis IN rather than ON their business.

Having established your enterprise, it is vital that you switch from IN to ON as soon as possible - it's the only way you will grow.

If you believe you are the only person who can do your job as well as you, you will only grow to the limit of your own capacity.

If you want your business to reach its full potential, you must hire others to work IN it … while you get ON with it!

5) Business Plans – Why?

I consider that your business plan must be part of your everyday thinking.

Some folks seem to think that a business plan is only needed for "special occasions" like raising more money or extending the overdraft and that for success all that is needed is some spreadsheets – the more complicated looking the better –a few colourful charts and some optimistic financial projections.

Sorry but NO!

You wouldn't expect the manager of your favourite sports team to stick to the same game plan each week.

You want them to adapt to the change in circumstance that playing a different team provides.

In our every changing business environment you must be adapting and refining your game – business - plan to ensure that you're the best that you can be, always.

I believe that your business plan needs to be a living working document which you update at least on a monthly basis.

6)   Businesses fail – why?

It's not a surprise that business development is relatively unsuccessful. There are so many areas a company needs to understand about its customers, the market, and their own behaviours.

Assumptions are often made about how competitors will behave, but often they don't do as predicted.

Firms spend scarce cash trying to grow their businesses through increasing market share, developing new products in existing markets, or entering new geographical markets for their current products.

We do much thoughtful internal planning, strategizing and talking, yet few of us get successful results. Why?

Experience shows me there are three recurring causes: the competitors don't behave as you expected, customers don't see the benefits, and crucially our businesses do not behave in the way our customers want!

Finally, if our way of working is not aligned with our business development plans, and with the customer's desired experience, success will be almost impossible to achieve.

7)   Can you cold call?

What are the things in your business that you don't like doing; but would not like to admit to others?

Chasing money?

Firing staff?

Talking to the bank manager?

For sure you can list others and I guess that somewhere will be, cold calling a potential customer.

For 99.9% with a small business this is the big one.

Most of us are uncomfortable with meeting strangers at the best of times, of trying to find a suitable opening gambit to the conversation and it's doubly difficult when we can't see the person.

Add to this the fear of rebuff – often from your target by a "gatekeeper" - and we all baulk, finding some other "busy" work to keep us from having to face what we believe is the inevitable rejection.

That call is the business of a group of extraordinary people with very singular skills.

Hire proven professional appointment makers.

8)   Don't stop believin'

The music fans amongst you will recall this is the title of the worldwide hit co-written by Neal Schon founder member of US band Journey.

The lyrics are about a young person setting out on the journey of life believin' in their dream and themselves.

Are you struggling with establishing your business?

Having sleepless nights wondering where the next order is going to come from?

Battling the lack of cash?

The doomsayers will be telling you that for every-body who makes it there are a thousand that don't, as the song says "some will win some will lose"

If you don't keep going when all seems lost, you'll never know if your dream idea works.

Please keep believin'. Because making the dream a success provides the most rewarding sense of satisfaction you will ever have when it is achieved for you and those close to you.

Remember "Never stop believing".

9)   Follow your dream

TV's music reality shows offer contestants a chance to act out their dreams and age is no barrier to taking part or to success.

Everybody, at least once in life, should live out their business dream and as in show business age is no obstacle.

After a number of false starts I finally became established in a sustainable successful enterprise in my late 40's.

The biggest problem you face in living out your dream is that the world is full of people telling you that you can't make it.

They will tell you variously that the markets too tough, the banks will never support you, you're not talented enough etc.

If you are considering following your dream, whatever your age, believe me living it out is one of the most rewarding things you will ever do.

The achievement of success for you and those close to you will bring a feeling of satisfaction that is huge.

10) Genuine management talent is scarce

Managers in your firm who have little or no real talent are those that deal with staff problems by bluster and coercion because they lack the courage to manage effectively.

Genuine management talent is scarce; my sense is that less than 10% of the workforce has the natural talent to manage others and of the 90% remaining I suspect that only 50% of them are sufficiently committed to be trained to some level of competency.

So, who are those talented enough to occupy the 10%?

They are the ones whose actions inspire folks on their Team, who confidently set down KPI's and then empathetically but firmly review these therefore developing talent.

When it comes to difficult times, they use skill and leadership to ensure that their Team overcomes adversity and significantly they make management decisions based not on office politics but on facts and what is best for their firm.

11) Heading for a wipe out?

Having a great year?

Got a full order book?

Desperately searching for new suppliers to keep up with demand for raw materials?

Scouring the lócal job market looking for new recruits?

Frankly, just busy as heck trying to run the business … right?

No time to think about marketing for the future, no time to get those changes done to the website, no time to get your "story" out on social media, no time to think about riding this crest to the next level by increasing your salesforce … right?

WRONG!

Prevaricate (or even worse, think that you don't need to do anything because this wave will last), and you are heading for a wipe out.

When the tide ebbs, the wave height drops, and the exhilaration of the crest recedes; the ride will be over.

Act now … prepare for the ebb while you are still riding the wave!

12) How exposed are you to your competition?

Very and always.

Right now, as you read this someone somewhere in the World is thinking about how to get an order from one of your biggest customers.

They are doing that hoping that you help them in their quest by being complacent – "our customers all know we are the best".

That your internet presence is not up to date and poor – "everybody in our key sectors knows we are here we – why keep telling them".

That you're pricing structure is out of date and not a reflection of real costs – "we don't have time (or is it the skill?) to negotiate with our key suppliers".

You are exposed 24/7 because the competition never ever goes away.

If you have lost an order you thought you should get in the last 3 months, it's because you let the competition win it by having thoughts and behaviours similar to those above.

13) How long is too long?

If you are spending 10% of your available selling time engaging with long term prospects – a subject addressed later on in "Time well spent? – then the question becomes how long should you spend pursuing a new prospect?

A businessman, let's call him "Fred", sees an opportunity to provide a service for an overseas client. Fred pitches his radically different approach.

The client contact rebuffs him and continues to provision the service from his own resources; whilst incidentally still purchasing other services from Fred.

Fred creates an opportunity at each review of the other services with the client contact, which changes over time, to reinforce his belief that his approach would be more cost effective and significantly increase his clients' market reach.

This negotiation lasts nine years; finally contact number three signs up.

How do I know that you can't specify exactly how long is too long? Because Fred was me.

14) How's your financial performance?

How often do you check your financial performance?

Is it once a year with your accountant/auditor?

Is it once a month with the bookkeeper?

Is it when you do the weekly accounts yourself?

Do you simply look at the bottom right-hand corner of the spreadsheet to see if the number is red or black?

If it's black, do you modestly give yourself a pat on the back and think that's OK then for another month?

If it's red, does instant panic set in and you issue memos urging everybody to watch/cut costs?

Looking at one type and set of data is useful – and certainly better than not looking at all.

However, your ability to manage your business will be radically improved if you use your accounts package to deliver informative trend reports and other data over multiple months.

Business wisdom develops best in the fertile soil of hindsight.

15) I could have been a contender

Said Marlon Brando's character ex-boxer Terry Malloy in "On the Waterfront"

Boxers come through the ranks fighting in front of small crowds. As they improve their record, the venues and purses get bigger, the people around them more numerous, and eventually they get the status of - contender. Now they need the teamwork to get that series of fights that puts them in the big time, with all the rewards that go with turning a contender into a Champion.

Has your business transitioned from a startup to the big time?

Have your team grown with the business?

Are you and they now at the top of your game?

Do your peers and competitors look at you and see a Star?

Or were you a contender, but didn't quite make it?

You reached for the stars but fell halfway?

Far better to have contended than to have been a mere spectator.

16) In Reverse

Traditional thinking says that you come up with an idea that you believe solves a problem, make a prototype or develop the drafts of a service, test the market, then work out how to deliver it profitably.

Then take it to potential customers who then buy or reject your solution to a problem that you believe they have.

I am certain that what we should do is start with the customer and work backwards towards a product or service.

Too often innovators waste time and valuable resources reconfiguring an idea based on test marketing results and/or internal discussions or simply a brainwave in the middle of the night which you think is utopia.

We should take our innate skills to a potential customer first and ask them what their current problems are to which they have no solution and then innovate an answer that meets their expectations.

17) It's our Destiny

When things go awry in business often the first response is for us to look for somebody to blame, someone to "pin" the responsibility for the screw up on.

The blame game always leads to anger (spoken or suppressed), and that leads to irate emails, cross words in the hallway, or withdrawal.

Where does that get us?

Frankly, not very far!

We need to take a frequent rain checks on our own role in why things have gone pear shaped perhaps the "process" was not robust enough, I didn't read the fine print of the contract or I just assumed that it wasn't relevant?

When we work out our own role in the problem, our tendency to blame diminishes, and our anger will dissipate.

We all (should) learn from these mistakes and move on; we are in control; it's our business and thus our own responsibility to shape our Destiny.

18) Is it too easy to communicate?

Once upon a time when you wanted to write to somebody you started with a blank piece of paper and a thought.

Today we have sophisticated software programs that offer all manner of templates, correct our grammar and spelling, help us to use words – in context – which we would never use in conversation; but look good on paper. We can cut and paste, merge with contact lists, personalize our salutations, add fancy watermarks and then send it by e mail to hundred's in an instant without having to lick a stamp.

Recently I had e mail business correspondence from three people I know well and who I speak to on a regular basis. In each case at first glance the letters appeared "personal" – they were not.

Technology has made us lazy.

A simple opening sentence that acknowledges the individuality of your relationship is all it takes to make it personal.

19) Light my Fire

In 1967, The Doors released the iconic "Light my Fire".

Does what you do every business day still light your fire?

Did you start a business or join a firm with the fire of passion coursing through your veins?

Have the flames died down?

Has it all gone quiet?

Do you now feel only the briefest sparks of interest?

Then it's time for a blast of the bellows – to rekindle the light and the heat from the dying embers.

Whilst it's true that you can't run a business or sustain a relationship on passion alone, it's equally true that without passion, indifference becomes the marker of both.

If your staff, your suppliers, and your customers sense your lack of passion for your products or your services, their enthusiasm will be diminished – and their eyes may well be attracted to the brighter lights of the fires of your competitors.

20) Market Information is King

The more I talk to folks, who "make" things, the more it's apparent that most have a fundamental lack of understanding of the "space" that they are operating in.

It seems that people rely for market information on gossip, innuendo, and uninformed chat.

This often from customers who are trying to ensure that they offer justification for their actions for not placing an order, driving the price down, changing the specs – all based on the "market".

Think of it like this – if you only read the gossip columns or look at Facebook or

Twitter to get your daily "news", then you will not be very informed about the world around you.

It's the same with your markets.

Get your informed market data from respected publications in the industry sectors you operate in and from the myriad of daily business news sources in print and online.

The informed make better business decisions.

21) Monthly Billing? Forget it

There really is no excuse for not invoicing your clients on time and frequently. What's wrong with traditional monthly billing you ask?

Lots.

In any business cash is King and the collection of it has become easier with simple to use modern software.

Ah! You say but I need to have all my supplier invoices, timesheets etc. in order to bill accurately so I do it all once a month usually late at night – stressed - after a long day managing the business.

I contend that the use of inexpensive software, that you get free training and support for, which tracks your open purchase orders and accurately allocates expenses to each client means that you can invoice more often and collect quicker.

Alternatively, delegate this task to the growing band of professional bookkeepers out there who will earn their fees in taking the stress away and improving the cash flow.

22) Never say NO!!

I heard the Director of a fabrication business say this a couple of weeks ago … "We couldn't possibly take on more work at present".

"Why ever not?" asked a fellow networker at their business-breakfast table.

"Well, we are really struggling to recruit; the workshop is flat out; etc., etc."

These kinds of statements are JUST PLAIN WRONG!

They are saying … "We are prepared to turn down profitable business."

DO WHAT???

All business is hard to get. Always take the order first … then figure out how to deliver! Don't give away business … it may be lost forever.

If you are struggling to recruit … look for smaller workshops where you can subcontract … ask folks in your supply chain who they would recommend.

And if you are at a network event, for heaven's sake don't moan – just ASK!

People love to work with other successful people.

23) Are you a Passive entrepreneur?

What you ask is a passive entrepreneur, how can you be inert, inactive or lethargic etc. and yet be a business mogul, tycoon or an impresario.

Well, you can't!

And yet I meet many people who are passive entrepreneurs, although entrepreneur is the word, they would use about themselves as a small businessperson who is about to start a business. It's not the word, without the adjective, that I would use.

Dictionary.com defines an entrepreneur as:

"a person who organizes and manages any enterprise ... usually with considerable initiative and risk".

Whilst many have great business ideas or wonderful inventions these never see the light of day because whilst they are adept at talking the talk, they fail to walk the walk of being entrepreneurial.

They spend their energy being passive because the reality of being entrepreneurial involves more commitment to initiative and risk than most are prepared to give.

24) Remember Where You Are

Recently while travelling on a train I overheard a conversation from across the aisle.

The two participants of the conversation joined the train approximately an hour from its destination. Once in their seats they picked up on an earlier dialogue.

They were unhappy with a client. Their views were various – the client clearly had not read their proposal, sent by e mail – the client just didn't understand the technology being offered, (by now I had a pretty good idea who they were) the inflection being "they are not as clever as we are". The timing of the meeting further irked them as it meant staying away.

Coincidentally when checking into my hotel the travellers were in front of me continuing their discourse on the hapless client.

Next morning, after a pre-meeting coffee with my client we entered his boardroom; I was not surprised to see the train travellers.

25) "Safe" or Talent.

Looking for a new member of the Team or to replace somebody?

Who leads the search? You? Your assistant? An outside agency?

Got a detailed job description?

Have you benchmarked the wage against the local market?

Searched your database of contacts for somebody who impressed you at some time? Asked key employees if they "know" anybody?

Or asked friends in pub?

Placed an ad in the local paper?

Whether you use any of the above or some other process one thing you must do is to ONLY hire the most talented person for the role.

Not the smartest dressed.

The one who you think you and everyone will like or worst of all.

The safe bet.

Managing talented people is a challenge but you must hire the person who brings talent to improve your company and the firm's offering to its customers.

Hiring safe is easy hiring talent takes nerve.

26) Same Old – Same Old

Sports coaches teach sound techniques and tell us that repeating them will give good results.

And in business if you repeat the good practises you will get the good result.

But when things aren't going well, we tend to ignore that advice and refuse to change our actions and persist with doing something which simply is not achieving the results we want.

We are having a difference of opinion with our minds.

Have you persisted with an advertising methodology knowing that its failing but not changed the way you promote your business?

Or carried on using a management technique or production process because "… we have always done it like that"

All classic Same Old Same Old mistakes!

When it's not going as you want it in business, its time go back to basics. Metaphorically returning to the sports coach and reminding ourselves of the fundamentals that made the business successful.

27) Set your prices based on your customers perception of value – not your own!

Your customers are unlikely to know neither your products cost base nor your profitability.

Thus, you should not restrict your mark ups to what you think customers think is reasonable.

It's vital that you know the costs of bringing your products the customer.

You should also know your competitions prices but best of all you should set your prices based on the customer's perception of value.

The key here is in order to achieve the later part of the last sentence you have to know accurately your costs.

If the customer perception of value is low and means that based on your cost base you will make a gross profit below your expected norm (or heaven forbid a loss!!) then your issue is now one of strategy and the medium to long term commercial benefit of the customer and your potential to up-sell them on other higher perceived value products.

28) Starting a Partnership? Be careful – very careful!

A friend recently approached me with the exciting news that he and a work colleague were going into partnership and wanted to know if I had any words of advice.

Yes, I said – 4

Be careful – very careful

And here are a further 108 to explain my warning.

Most partnerships start in a euphoric blaze of goodwill

And a large majority of these partnerships will be 50/50.

WRONG!

Why you say, "we will never fall out" "we trust each other" "we couldn't do this without each other" Really?

As businesses mature and personal circumstances change – as they inevitably will – you will have differences of opinion and in a 50/50 partnership there is no arbiter.

A simple answer is to make it 49/49 and give 1% each to trusted business advisors and draw up your shareholder agreement so that they have the power to adjudicate in the event of an impasse.

29) Status Quo – the management meeting challenge

Are your management meetings challenging and forward thinking or like a concert from veteran British rock band Status Quo?

Everybody drifts in; the chatter gets louder as the start time goes by, till the venue is packed.

The band sweep on stage

The CEO and CFO arrive.

The concert starts with 2 old favourites

The secretary reads the minutes.

Then its 2 numbers from the forthcoming album

Talk of trade show attendance or perhaps a new customer.

Now it's a medley of the band's greatest hits The team again discusses why Caroline in accounts isn't more helpful and of course the big number 1 why sales don't understand production.

For the finale the CEO asks for more effort with backing from the CFO's well-rehearsed encore about costs.

Both audiences felt comfortable and leave satisfied.

That's fine for Quo but for you to be number 1 you must challenge the "Status Quo".

30)   Success is not a divine right

Achievement in your chosen business is not a divine right.

Achievements through the efforts of you and others should be seen as being a rental.

And it's a rent that must be earned and paid to ensure you keep your eyes on the prize of success.

Often, we see firms both large and small become successful and then slowly fade away to become also rans or worst still end up fighting for their very existence.

In almost all the cases that I have studied the root cause can be found in the firm's management becoming distracted from that prize that comes from executing a profitable business plan.

Distractions takes many forms; surprisingly it can frequently be traced back to them being really successful – they believed it was a divine right and forgot payment of the rent has to be a daily effort by all; that's focused on the prize.

31) Taking Flight

There are 3 striking similarities between butterflies and successful businesses.

1) Successful businesses evolve through a metamorphosis that parallels the butterfly. Conception (egg) development (larva) fundraising (pupa) and go to market (adult) at each step a different objective or resource are required.

   Larva, like development, consume lots of food; the adult must reproduce to complete the lifecycle just as successful businesses must replicate their product or service in order to stay profitable.

2) As with the butterfly successful business leaders are often colourful, able to alight on a problem then feed on the nectar of the issue, draw energy from solving the situation and move on.

3) Butterflies are often seen "puddling" where a number of them get together to feed on nutrients to build up strength.

All smart leaders should do something similar, meet with others to share and learn and then take flight again stronger and better prepared.

32) Time well spent? Part One

Are you a small-business owner?

Does running your business take up to 60 hours a week of your time?

Have you questioned how you allocate those hours to:

1) Managing/Leading?

2) Making/Delivering?

3) Selling/Marketing?

Is it equal time on each?

Do you spend the majority of your time making/delivering?

If you've answered yes to either of the above, your business is at risk.

Managing/Leading the business should take no more than 10% (6 hours) of your time ... any more than that means you're doing "busy work" and should hire an administrator.

Making/Delivering your products or services should take no more than 35% (21hours) of your time ... more than that and you don't trust the staff that you hired.

Absent a focus of at least 55% (33 hours) of your time on Selling/Marketing, you'll soon have nothing to manage, lead, make, or deliver – and be broke.

33) Time well spent? Part Two

A young salesperson of my acquaintance enthusiastically told me how busy they were dashing from one meeting to another, chasing after new clients – a reminder of my younger self!

To good salespeople, the thrill of the chase always pumps the adrenaline, making it a challenge to balance the allocation of time and resources.

In the previous story I suggested a guideline for small business owners on how to allocate their time spent per week on Managing (10%), Making (35%), and Selling (55%).

I'd suggest that these very same percentage allocations could help that young salesperson maintain a balance of focus in their efforts:

10% on long term prospects

35% on high potential prospects

55% on existing, invoice-paying clients.

If you're involved in sales, it's easy to be blinded by the exciting lights of new clients … and just as easy to forget those paying your current invoices!

34) To state the blindingly obvious

Mankind does not apparently learn from the experiences of the past, whether that's in politics, business or life in general!

Ah you say "Of course; we know that!" History repeats itself.

There's no fool like an old fool.

I am sure you have similar clichés. So why is it that we humans don't absorb the knowledge from earlier experiences, understand it and then act on it?

Well, we are all taught that practise make perfect (another cliché!) so we seem wired to repeat the "mistake" rather than accept it's an error and find a different way to do it.

Too often we analyse the result of the error and try rearranging the existing practise for a different outcome.

Disastrous!

In your business your best friend in combating a repeat of history and being an old fool is a blank white board, a clear schedule and an obvious changed viewpoint.

35) Too "posh" to talk?

You have climbed the ladder of success and reached your personal/professional summit.

The bright idea that morphed into a start-up became a profitable firm.

The young person who joined a company came through the ranks to a senior position.

Perhaps you took over a moribund organisation and turned it around.

From small beginnings where you did everything, took every call answered every e mail there's now a plethora of folks who do that mundane stuff.

On the rise to success and recognition you interacted with people who in various ways were the rungs in your ladder to the top, providing sales leads, opening "doors" or simply being there for you.

Becoming remote, too important or too busy to return their calls or e mails, runs the risk of them removing their rung, too many removals jeopardies the ladders' integrity and therefore the collapse of your reputation and possibly your business.

36)   Too small to bother with?

In recent weeks we have had some examples of poor customer service.

From a top 10 firm in the world.

By a franchisee for a national company.

And a small local business.

In each case these firms have been in our supply chain for ten to twenty years.

Whilst we are disappointed about the level of service from the two larger businesses, they will survive without us – the small local business does give cause for concern.

We started using them soon after they were formed and whilst they weren't the cheapest, supporting local small firms seemed the right thing to do.

As sales and the size of their clients have climbed, a familiarity has bred disdain – made clear in attitudes and incidents which showed that our account was considered too small to bother with.

On the way up the ladder, you can't afford to destroy the rungs "beneath" you.

37) Wannabe

What do you want what do you really really want?

(with thanks to the Spice Girls)

You're a service provider and have recently been appointed to a role with responsibility for business development.

Or perhaps even more exciting, you have set up your own firm.

You "wannabe" successful early on (just like the Spice Girls were).

You want an order that vindicates others' belief in you, whether that's your directors, investors, or your supportive family.

On the weekend you get a text from a longtime customer you handled in your previous job. The message states that they have a requirement that in your new role you can satisfy.

What you don't know from the message is the quantum of the request.

There is no legal constraint on you contacting this potential customer.

So, what would you choose?

To "really, really wannabe" a success … and call the contact straight away to establish the requirement?

Or will you be the other "wannabe" … and wait till Monday?

38   A waste of time!

A client asked me to source a fabricator for a potential order that they lacked the capacity to fill.

I visited a firm recommended to me, scoped out their capabilities, and had discussions on deal structure.

I drafted a commercial agreement, and my client couriered drawings for pricing.

In response the MD requested funding of additional capital equipment (not unusual).

This was agreed.

I estimated their costs for providing the quotation at £8,750 (0.00175% of the potential order).

They have sales of £5m/year. The value of the order to be placed was £5m over 2 years – an increase in sales of 50%/year.

When the order did not materialise, the MD claimed the exercise was a "Waste of Time".

Any opportunity to increase sales should always be viewed as time well spent, not wasted – when it comes at minimal cost and provides additional capital equipment it's a no brainer!

39) What Lawyers can teach us about selling

No successful courtroom lawyer is an expert in all the circumstances that they are called upon to represent.

What they do is bring the facts together and present them in a way that convinces the Judge and/or Jury of the validity of their client's case.

To achieve this, they are supported by all the members of the team back in the office - paralegals, researchers, deposition writers, administrators, etc., to bring about the right result for their client.

In the same way, it's the responsibility of every member of your business to ensure that they support the person in the sales role by doing everything within their area of expertise to ensure delivery of the client's requirements.

Then, like the courtroom lawyer, it takes someone who can harness the expertise of the team and can use their skills to present your offering in a manner that the client finds irresistible.

40) What sort of salesperson should represent you?

For the moment please don't think about you or anybody in your firm who carry's the title salesman but instead think of people in your social circle you know who do that job for others.

What do you see?

"A chatty man"

"A bit of a smarty pants"

"A smooth talker"

"A loose cannon"

In other words, the usual stereotypes!

All the successful salesmen I have met were none of these things.

However, they all had the following attributes:

Great listeners,

Were known for their integrity,

Could execute the sales process with clarity for the customer and the business,

Strong personalities with good social skills who had a presence that represented their company in a manner that made customers want to do business with them.

And above all they had the mental fortitude to accept that, as in sport, in sales you don't score with every swing of the bat.

41) Where do you go from here?

When a friend went to work for a small family business in his 20's he had not much thought about eventually owning it.

Some years later now nearing his 60th birthday and as the sole shareholder he wanted to know what to do next.

The first obvious piece of advice is all businesses should have an exit strategy in place from the get-go if you too have his situation but are still in your 30's or 40's then don't wait!

How you exit a business will be predicated on your business model but as a general rule of thumb I suggest you get your external accountants to put together a brief offering document.

This must focus on what you have to sell and promote a realistic valuation.

Then get their help to gauge where your value is relative to others in similar situation.

With this done you are now prepared to canvas opportunities.

42) Who sets the "tone" in your business?

Who's the voice of your business?

You? Sales? Production?

When the phone rings, who picks up the call?

None of the above? Someone in admin? The latest junior?

What training were they given?

With the advent of direct dial (press 1 for sales, 2 for etc), of the ubiquitous mobile, of instant communication by email and social media, it seems that the customer who calls your "switchboard" has become an afterthought.

It is always irritating (and sometimes downright annoying!) to be greeted by a voice who clearly has no idea of (or any interest in) who you are or how long you have been a customer, and who insists on asking the universal "Can you tell me what it's in connection with …".

How difficult can it be to spend some time training ALL of your staff in the meaning of your business and the value of your key clients?

43) You're never off duty

A friend was recently driving in London and was cut off by a van bearing the logo of a firm offering the design, manufacture and installation of chimney liners.

My female friend, somewhat aggrieved at the behaviour of the driver, vigorously sounded her horn.

At the next traffic light when she pulled up alongside, she received a torrent of sexist abuse before the van took off.

This friend has recently bought an old house as a restoration project, which includes the lining of four substantial Georgian chimneys.

Having made a note both of the van number and the company's contact details, she researched the firm, found an email address for the CEO, and sent a note explaining why she would not be seeking a quotation from his firm.

If you advertise – in any form – *it's an absolute necessity to ensure that all members of the firm represent the brand positively.*

44) Eliminate the impossible

You and your Team are wrestling with a problem; a problem that you are all agreed is having a major impact on your business. Everybody's doing analysis; reporting back, there are innumerable ad hoc discussions going on and yet nothing seems to answer the problem.

The more you pour over the issue and the more ideas come to the fore the more confused everybody becomes!

One solution is to use a mechanism that some police forces use when investigating serious crimes; that I have adapted.

Use two white boards that are readily accessible by the entire Team, mark one at the top with Impossible and the other with Possible.

Next ask everybody over a period of say 2 days to put on the Impossible board those ideas that they believe won't solve the problem.

Having cleared everybody's mind you and they are now free to fill in the Possible board.

45) One Day at A Time

Do you dream of being a rock star or a power-ful politician? Maybe a leading academic? Per-chance an Oscar winning actor, a great leader of your chosen faith?

Possibly making millions inventing "The Next Big Thing"?

But you haven't achieved any of these yet, and if you're honest with yourself, it doesn't look as though you will.

I'm not against ambition - indeed I've been ambi-tious all my life.

But there is a silent danger in daydreaming about what is currently out of reach.

It deflects your mind away from using the talents that you already have and maximising them to the best effect.

Each day brings fresh opportunities for you to "strut your stuff" - doing what you do well, stretch-ing the skills that you have, being the very best that you can be – here and now.

Leave the future to take care of itself – it will surprise you.

46) Opportunity is everywhere

Its late in the day and your flight has already been delayed, when the gate staff announce a further delay. In exasperation the person next to you mutters a profanity and then instantly apologies!

You strike up a conversation about the frustrations of business travel and swap stories.

The airline cancels your flight; you collect accommodation and food vouchers, share a cab to a hotel and arrange to meet for dinner.

Over dinner you discover that your companion is involved in supplying services to a company, in your destination city, that you have had difficulty securing an order from. Further discussion reveals that the person you really need to be talking to is the same person that your new friend deals with.

They make an introduction and later the next day you take an initial order.

Not all business comes through traditional marketing pathways.

Any conversation can lead to opportunity.

47) It shouldn't be you.

Over 40+ years lots of clients I worked with were owner operators.

Many believed that they were the only person who knew enough about their business's innovations/ technology to be able to "sell" them.

If there is one thing 40 + years has taught me it's that in 90% of cases this statement is just not true.

Because 9 out of 10 of us find rejection in any part of our lives difficult to take; doubly so if we think it's is aimed at something, we hold dear, the product or service we have developed - our "baby" – it's tough to take, so we take steps to avoid the rejection by:

- not asking for the order directly

- not calling the client

- not making an appointment to follow up

- or simply spending more time "tweaking" the product

However small your firm be sure the right person is responsible for selling your "baby".

48) Closing that sale

Only 1 in 3 presentations result in closing the sale.

Therefore, the skill of closing of that sale is paramount.

This next statement, many of you will believe is wrong; but in-depth product knowledge and/or industry experience is not the number one nor only skill set needed for closing a sale.

I believe that it takes something called **FPER**:

Fortitude - Strength and firmness of mind.

Concentration is vital so as to not be "blown" off course

Preparation - Being ready beforehand – not "winging it".

Plan the presentation to give you the best chance of success.

Engagement – Ability to captivate the client.

Your body language has to say "I'm enjoying this"

Rehearsal - Practicing in preparation for what is a "public" performance.

You are frequently in front of more than one person who is comfortably sitting in their own space.

As such you are akin to a performer stepping on stage.

49) Reaching new markets

Developing opportunities in new markets always seems to take twice as long and cost twice as much as you first thought!

So how do you go about finding the time and devoting the resources to reach out into new markets without risking your current sales?

1. Put together a simple research plan to identify potential targets, sectorial and geographical using the power of the internet, then-and this is vital- budget the time and costs for carrying out more detailed research.

2. With your target markets identified talk to your business network contacts about their experiences in those markets.

3. Additionally, the list of Government bodies offering help is mind numbing along with the private firms available for hire.

4. Finally, if in any doubt about a market and its opportunities stop and look elsewhere because accepting something that's second best just to try a new market will end in tears.

50)   The Raft of Life

Busy doing busy work?

Working all hours, the Almighty sends?

Concentrating on squeezing the last preverbal pip of costs out of your business?

Making sure that everybody is performing to your expectations?

In other words, you're absorbed by things in your immediate sphere.

Like the lone survivor of a shipwreck holding on grimly to the life raft desperate to survive and who, in their anxiety, forget to look around therefore missing the passing ship that is their one opportunity for survival.

In your business life how often have you missed an opportunity to further yourself or your firm because you failed to look up from your raft to spot that big sales order, that person who could make a difference, the investment that would create opportunity ....or on a personal level, the role that would transform your career?

Often that seminal moment in life is just a head turn away.

51) No man is an island

"No man is an Island" wrote John Donne and yet too many firms – in particular those of an engineering persuasion and equally those who are often referred to as SME's operate as though they are.

Do you only have external interaction day to day when a customer or supplier wants to talk to you?

Is that because you have a shallow database of clients with perhaps one or two big customers who dominate every day?

Do you find it difficult even impossible to reach out to new customers?

You are not alone - the fear of rejection is not something many of us can live with.

So, try this. Partnering.

Look at your customer's products and then find those who supply non-competitive parts to the same product and partner together to maximise sales with that client and together then reach out to similar clients; supporting each other makes it easier.

52) It's not where you've come from ...

I was brought up in a farming community and studied agriculture. After graduating I spent the next 7 years in various jobs in and around the farming industry.

By age 23 I had learnt that, in a variety of scenarios, I could sell or perhaps more accurately put I could "close".

Since then, I have spent my commercial life "closing" transactions across the World and in all manner of industrial sectors, hotels, storage systems, construction projects, transport, job creation, leisure projects plus of course consulting assignments! I haven't invented anything. I am not an engineer, technician, accountant, academic, or an administrator.

However, I have spent a lifetime learning the skill of how best to present to others in order to get them to accept my proposal – be that on behalf of a client or myself.

To close the deal.

Be that a company restructure or simply hiring the right consultant!

53) … but Dad you were a hooker …

A firm builds lasting success when the skills of all are welded together into an effective team.

Skills are best coached by those who understand the nuances of the role, and how best it fits the overall aims of the firm.

Team sports, where specialist coaches work with players who have different roles within the team, provide an excellent template. In football, the goalkeeping coach doesn't show strikers how to score goals.

In cricket, the batting coach can't introduce bowlers to the dark arts of bowling.

Yet so often in business, I come across people with key skills who are reporting to (and led by!) those with contrary skills and responsibilities e.g., Sales to Accounts, Operations to Marketing, IT to HR.

To return to the sports analogy, that is like a parent who was a rugby hooker hollering advice from the touchline to their child, who is a star winger

54) To move or not to move

It is unusual in team sports that athletes spend their whole careers with one Team.

Indeed, football stars move with regularity either following a favourite coach or to a Team where they believe greater success and financial rewards lie.

In business it's equally unusual for any of us to stay with the same firm or in the same industry for an entire career.

As with athletes our moves are often influenced by other people who we trust or have perhaps grown not to!

Or by the belief that we are undervalued in our role and a new field will provide opportunity for both greater job satisfaction and financial security.

But a word of caution, as many a football player has found out, whilst the field you are currently playing on may look a bit brown and beaten up the new field may not be the colour you thought it was!

55) Being contrary is being smart

How often have you been frustrated when some-body in the business or for that matter in life in general seems to be taking an outlier position on an issue when you are sure that they are only do-ing it to be "difficult"?

Perhaps they are not being difficult but smart.

In my youth I took part in public speaking contests and enjoyed involvement in debating societies; of-ten we were deliberately asked to present a mo-tion from a point of view we would normally not share.

This taught us to understand the contrary position.

And over the years I have used this device as an effective management tool.

Getting folks to argue the opposite point of view gives them an appreciation of the overall argu-ment and makes them better prepared to make their own case.

Those who can see and understand the whole picture will always win the argument.

Part 2 - Thoughts

1. Yesterday-History. Today-Discovery. Tomorrow-Mystery.

2. Whilst keeping your feet firmly on Mother Earth, don't forget to look up to see Mother Nature around you.

3. 70% intuition 30% logic is a good recipe for making great decisions.

4. Your reputation is your shield against the slings and arrows of tough times.

5. Don't look behind you - you're not going there, and you will likely trip on old mistakes.

6. The ascent to success takes many hard steps … but the descent to failure is swift.

7. People fear and misunderstand dreamers, but never be afraid of your dream.

8. Begin again.

9. Discipline, Patience, Concentration.

10. To make a living doing what you love is a gift which is freely available to us all, if we search diligently.

11. It takes courage to grow up and be what we want to be.

12. Never pass up on talent. If you do, others will benefit.

13. You do you.

14. The similarity between integrity and virginity is remarkable - once lost, it is never recovered.

15. Actions escape from the words of a plan - that's both their purpose and their majesty.

16. Things that seem impossible to others are the norm for you. That's genius.

17. A bad day has ended but remember there will be a new tomorrow.

18. However long and dark the night, there is always the dawn.

19. Treat people as if they have already reached their potential.

20. A talented person can frequently hit their chosen target. Genius hits targets others can't see.

21. Success isn't given ... it is earned.

22. Procrastination is fear by another name.

23. You find new ways to win by having losses along the way.

24. The measure of a parent's success is how much their children surpass them.

25. The wise will always demonstrate their wisdom by their answers, some can only demonstrate their cleverness by the questions they ask.

26. Success isn't yours by divine right. It's leased to you by the efforts of yourself and others, and payment on that lease is due every day.

27. Better to be disliked for who you are, than to be liked for somebody you are not.

28. Dreams don't come with a price list - so the bigger the better.

29. Blunt pencils make poor writing implements - so sharpen frequently for clear script. Your brain is no different.

30. Your legacy leaves the footprints that guide the paths for others.

31. Every decision should pass the 6 months test i.e., will this still look good in 6 months? If in doubt, it's probably the wrong decision.

32. Meaningful stories well told light the fires that fuel your passion.

33. Good managers in your business are like mint chocolates – one is never enough.

34. You wouldn't ask your Doctor to service your car, your tailor to re-wire your house or salesperson to design a road bridge, so why expect an engineer to increase your sales.

35. Never deceive yourself, or others, by attempting a task for which you have no skill.

36. Simply to be intelligent is of no value to you or others if you don't practise it and then apply it.

37. Integrity in business may not win you hundreds of friends, but those it does will be worthwhile.

38. To accept a compromise you must first fully understand the other party's point of view. Anything less is acquiescence.

39. Never negotiate your integrity.

40. To take the first step you don't have to be able to see the top of the mountain.

41. Glider pilots are aware of the unseen thermals that lift them to new heights – some call this "flying by the seat of your pants". In business, learn to be aware of the positive actions and input of others around you - that will lift your performance to new heights too.

42. A well-defined structure in any business is best achieved by using the K.I.S.S principle – keep it simple stupid!

43. Business culture eats business strategy for breakfast – everyday.

44. Don't be what people say you should be, be what your heart tells you to be.

45. Hindsight is useless if you didn't have the foresight to set your sights on something in front of you.

46. Want to control this year's costs? Then you should have planned for it last year.

47. Living in the past means staying in the past.

48. Plan your business for the next 5 years assuming you won't be there tomorrow.

49. Age or seniority may give you wisdom – but it doesn't give you the right to be right.

50. Do you sometimes feel as though you're in a tribute band, simply playing the same old song written by somebody else? Then strike out and form your own band.

51. Leadership is about being decisive, committed and sure of your position - but most of all its about others - not you.

52. Your passion is the defender of your faith.

53. Every day offers the prospect of you being the best that you can be. Every day.

54. Its easy to fall from even the most modest of heights if you don't concentrate.

55. Your beliefs and the things you stand for are more visible to others than you.

56. Running a successful business is based on a series of associations or partnerships - but one thing it's not – it's not a democracy.

57. Strong friendships take time to build, but trust can be forged in a moment.

58. A career politician thinks about the next election. A statesman thinks about the next generation.

59. Never confuse a project spreadsheet profit for the real thing.

60. Don't blame your staff for poor execution of your brilliant business plan - question the plan itself.

61. Never arrive at work with the same thoughts you left with last night.

62. It's not the years of service in your job that counts - it's the quality of the service in your years.

63. Companies don't fail because they are wrong, they fail because of lack of commitment.

64. Giving back helps others to move forward.

65. Life may not be a dress rehearsal - but practising your best presentation everyday can only make it better.

66. Structure follows strategy.

67. To achieve success, what you stop is just as important as what you do.

68. The facts are the facts - everything else is human interpretation.

69. Any road will get you where you want to go if you don't know where you are going.

70. There will never be another Churchill, Mandela, Elvis, or Pele ... so be your own unique self.

71. It is said that impersonation is the highest form of flattery. So, flatter yourself by being yourself.

72. Don't try to be somebody because all the somebodies are already taken. Be you.

73. Practise it is said makes perfect. Make sure your practises are not simply repetition of mistakes you've made before.

74. Be careful working for friends ... a feeling of betrayal is never far away.

75. A business owner that lacks passion is simply a manager.

76. As the owner or shareholder of a business, never look on yourself as an employee.

77. Had a great year? Got a full order book? Busy running the business?
Now's the time to do more marketing.
Now's the time to refresh the website and your social media presence. Now's the time to take on extra salespeople.
Not when the opposite is true.

78. In sport you may not know all the rules, but you still play. In business it's just the same, you won't ever understand all the nuisances of the regulations around your chosen field, but you still can give it your best.

79. The sword of truth is both difficult to say and to bear. Make your use of it swift and sharp.

80. It's not the employer who pays the wages. They only handle the money.
It's your customers who pay the wages.

81. Never scorn small beginnings. Remember the majority of big companies started somewhere on a kitchen table.

82. Have expectations of yourself and you will do exceptional things.

83. Live for today. Tomorrow is promised to no-one.

84. Never save something for a special occasion; everyday of your life is a special occasion.

85. To stay sharp at work, develop an interest away from work. that doesn't compete for your passion at work.

86. If you believe you are the star performer in a poor company, what are you doing about it?

87. When bringing something new to the market, no amount of studies, computer analysis, or market research can substitute for the test of reality.

88. Going down with a sinking ship is damaging to your financial health.

89. The financial success of your business can only be accomplished alongside the development of your Team.

90. You have to hunt success. It won't find you.

91. As your income grows - so must you.

92. To go far you have to dare to be different.

93. When travelling on a ship that's in troubled waters – make sure you have a firm grip on the helm.

94. Thinking of buying another business? It's not synergy that counts – it's contribution!

95. However elusive it may be the pursuit of perfection is admirable.

96. When hiring only select the candidate that has proven they can do the job - not someone you think can do it.

97. Concerned about the course you're on? You can't change the wind that's blowing you along, but you can change the set of your sails for a different course.

98. When you reach the top of the mountain there's even less room for error.

99. As in sport, politics, and entertainment, in business only the very few reach the top.

100. It's not your costs that should set your price list. Its your customer's perception of value of your goods, products or services.

101. What you earn you deserve.

102. If everything is equal the simple solution is the best answer.

103. Whatever your position in your organization, ask yourself every day "what has been my contribution"?

104. Reminiscing about your past successes is not only good for the ego it also builds confidence that you can repeat it in the future.

105. When viewing any issue (personal, business or political), the lens of perspective is vital to ensure balance.

106. The abiding impression others have of you is measured by the footprints you leave on the landscape of their lives.

107. A manager with passion must be nurtured and valued.

108. Intuition can't be learned, like skateboarding or golf, by watching others. But it's vital for navigating life's highway.

109. Starting a business is frequently a personal option. It's an obligation that you make it a success for those for whom you are responsible.

110. If you are going backwards in your business don't keep your foot on the accelerator.

Acknowledgements

To all the past clients, work mates and employers, I have worked with and who taught me the skills and understandings that have translated into this offering, you will never fully realize the impact you had on my journey.

You are too many to mention here but I hope some of you recognise in these pages not only yourselves but the shared experiences that we had!

To the colleagues in Pathfinder Team Consulting who took a ride back in 1990 on an idea nobody had tried before; thank you for your faith and of course your excellent work across dozens of different industry sectors on four continents.

To JR Reed for the original idea for this "book". A former client and for the last 20 years a friend who enjoys life in a city I grew to love, New Orleans.

To Thomas Kelly for encouragement and correcting my English (difficult for any Scotsman - particularly one living in Canada) but most importantly for editing and making sense of my stories and thoughts. Whilst on the subject of editing etc. thanks go to Nick Caya and his Team at word 2 kindle based in Virginia Beach without whom you would not be reading this!

To Mark Peters who first insisted I had something to say on business to a wider audience and gave me a slot on his radio station to prove it. Once he became involved in this project, he changed my approach and that led to a soon to be released audio download based on this e book.

To my wife Mai, who has lived with me in four different countries and first encouraged me, whilst we were living in France, to follow my ultimate dream. Through all the ups and downs of helping me run our own "shop" she unwaveringly supported me. Without that encouragement for the last nearly 40 years success for myself and the consulting business would have been impossible and thus, this handbook would not have been written.

And finally, to my children, grandchildren and great grandchildren, I hope that you glean something from here that helps you in your very varied careers to grow and then take the opportunity to follow your dreams to become successful, on your terms, for you and your families.